# Wetland Animals

Written by Deborah Hodge
Illustrated by Pat Stephens

Kids Can Press

# For Emily, a nature lover, who kayaks along the shores of many wonderful wetlands — D.H.

# For Nickie — P.S.

I would like to gratefully acknowledge the thorough review of the manuscript and art by Dr. Diane Srivastava, Associate Professor (Ecology), Zoology Department, University of British Columbia, Vancouver, BC.

Thank you also to my talented editors Sheila Barry and Lisa Tedesco for their valuable help with this series.

Kids Can Press acknowledges the financial support of the Government of Ontario, through the Ontario Media Development Corporation's Ontario Book Initiative; the Ontario Arts Council; the Canada Council for the Arts; and the Government of Canada, through the BPIDP, for our publishing activity.

Published in Canada by
Kids Can Press Ltd.
29 Birch Avenue
Toronto, ON  M4V 1E2

Published in the U.S. by
Kids Can Press Ltd.
2250 Military Road
Tonawanda, NY  14150

www.kidscanpress.com

Kids Can Press is a Corus™ Entertainment company

Edited by Lisa Tedesco and Sheila Barry
Designed by Kathleen Gray
Printed and bound in Singapore

The paper used to print this book was produced with elemental chlorine-free pulp, harvested from managed sustainable forests.

The hardcover edition of this book is smyth sewn casebound. The paperback edition of this book is limp sewn with a drawn-on cover.

CM 08  0 9 8 7 6 5 4 3 2 1
CM PA 08  0 9 8 7 6 5 4 3 2 1

**Library and Archives Canada Cataloguing in Publication**
Hodge, Deborah
    Wetland animals / written by Deborah Hodge ; illustrated by Pat Stephens.

(Who lives here?)
ISBN 978-1-55453-045-8 (bound)
ISBN 978-1-55453-046-5 (pbk.)

1. Wetland animals—Juvenile literature.  I. Stephens, Pat, 1950–
II. Title.  III. Series: Hodge, Deborah.  Who lives here?

QL113.8.H63 2008        j591.768        C2007-905564-8

# Contents

# What Are Wetlands?

Wetlands are lands that are covered by shallow water some or all of the time, such as swamps, ponds, bogs or marshes. Wetlands are found across the world, in hot and cool areas.

This pond is in a cool part of the world. Like all wetland creatures, pond animals have bodies built for living in or near the water.

Wetland animals also live in hot places. The Bengal tiger slinks through steamy swamps, hunting for food. Roar!

The platypus swims in rivers and lakes in a warm, southern area. It digs a home in the riverbank with its sharp claws.

Wetland plants, such as cattails, grow in wet soil or water. Animals eat the plants or make homes among them.

# Hippopotamus

The hippopotamus is one of the biggest animals on Earth!
An adult can weigh as much as four heavy pianos.

Hippos cool off in rivers and lakes in hot parts of the world. At night,
they go to shore to gobble up tasty grasses. Munch, munch!

A hippo pokes its snout out of the water to breathe when the rest of its body is underwater.

Hippos have long, thick teeth for fighting other hippos or attacking crocodiles that threaten their babies.

If the river or lake dries up, a hippo takes a mudbath to protect its sensitive skin from the hot sun.

# Mallard Duck

The mallard duck flies fast and swims well. Mallards nest on the shores of cool ponds and lakes in many regions.

These soft, fuzzy ducklings hatched from eggs their mother laid. The tiny babies can swim right away. Quack, quack!

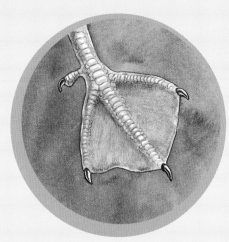

Big webbed feet work like paddles to push the duck through the water.

A duck rubs its feathers with oil from a gland near its tail. With this waterproof coat, the duck stays warm and dry!

Bottoms up! A hungry mallard tips upside down to nibble on tasty plants and small creatures underwater.

# Capybara

The gentle capybara is about the size of a pig. Capybaras wander through warm wetlands near forests and grass.

Living in a family group helps the capybaras stay safe from hungry jaguars. If danger is near, a capybara will bark like a dog. Ruff!

Capybara mothers care for all the babies in the group and take turns feeding them.

Adults eat grasses and water plants. Long front teeth cut the food, and flat back teeth chew it.

A capybara's eyes sit high on its head. This helps it watch for enemies as it swims.

# Bullfrog

The bullfrog has big, bulging eyes and soft, slippery skin. Bullfrogs live at the edges of cool ponds and rivers.

Splish, splash! The bullfrog is a powerful swimmer. It pushes through the water with its long, strong legs and wide, webbed feet.

This is a baby frog or tadpole. Its tail will shrink and legs will grow as it changes into an adult frog. Croak!

A hungry bullfrog gobbles up almost anything it can find — worms, insects, snakes, fish and even other frogs!

A bullfrog doesn't need to drink. It takes in water through its skin.

# Crocodile

The fierce crocodile prowls through wetlands in hot parts of the world. Crocodiles roar like lions!

A crocodile silently floats and watches for prey — the fish, birds, zebras, antelopes and other animals it hunts. Suddenly, it attacks!

Chomp! The crocodile grabs the prey with its powerful jaws and razor-sharp teeth.

Baby crocodiles hatch from eggs laid on shore. Their mother gently carries them to the water, where she can watch over them.

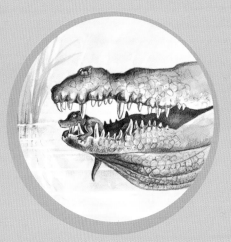

Strong, sturdy legs help a crocodile move fast on land. Sharp claws are good for climbing up hills.

# Beaver

The beaver is a fast, graceful swimmer. Beavers live in cool ponds, lakes and rivers close to wooded areas.

Beavers build a cozy home, called a lodge, from trees and branches they cut down. Tiny baby beavers are born inside the lodge.

A baby beaver drinks its mother's milk. The baby cries when it's hungry and coos when it's full. Coo, coo …

Iron in a beaver's teeth makes them strong and orange. Beavers eat tree bark. Crunch!

A beaver's webbed feet push it forward as it swims. Its big, flat tail works like an oar to help it steer.

# Flamingo

The elegant flamingo wades in the water on its long legs. Flamingos flock in shallow, salty wetlands in hot regions.

Many thousands of flamingos gather together. Their pink color comes from the tiny plants and shrimp they feed on.

Slurp! A hungry flamingo sucks in water, then squirts it out. Bristles in its beak catch bits of food as the water flows by.

A baby's beak isn't ready to filter food, so the parents feed the chick a special red "milk" made inside their bodies.

Whoosh! Big, wide wings make the flamingo a strong flier. Flamingos travel from one feeding place to another.

# Anaconda

The anaconda is as long as a bus and as heavy as two big men. Anacondas swim in rivers and swamps in hot areas.

The water holds up the anaconda's heavy body as it drifts and waits for a thirsty deer, capybara or other animal to come near.

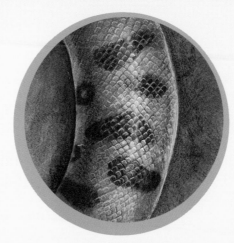

Spotted green skin blends in with the color of water plants and helps the snake hide.

The anaconda coils its powerful body around its prey and squeezes tight. The snake will swallow it whole. Gulp!

Hours after baby anacondas are born, they can swim and hunt on their own.

# Moose

The powerful moose is taller than a large horse. Moose roam through cool, swampy wetlands near forests.

A baby moose, called a calf, grows quickly on its mother's milk. The mother munches on water plants — her favorite summer food.

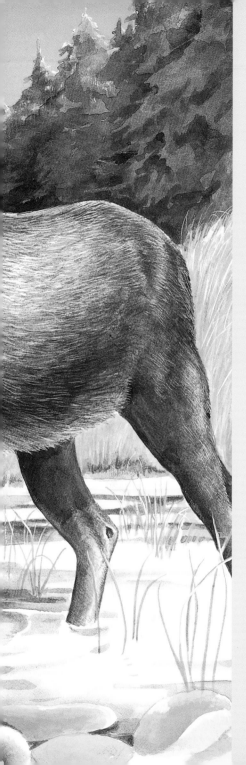

Moose are strong swimmers. A calf can run fast and swim well a few days after it is born.

A male moose has huge antlers. Males battle with their antlers to see who is the strongest. Crash! Crack!

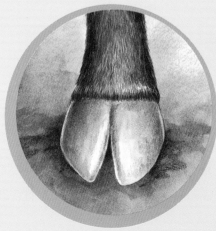

A moose's big hooves spread wide to keep it from sinking into the soggy ground.

# Animal Words

Every wetland animal has special body parts that help it get food and stay safe in its watery home. Can you find pictures of these body parts in the book?

**beak**
page 19

**foot**
page 9

**hoof**
page 23

**skin**
page 21

**snout**
page 7

**teeth**
page 17

## For Parents and Teachers

Wetlands are found on every continent except Antarctica. Inland wetlands have fresh water, while coastal wetlands have salt or brackish (mixed) water. Wetlands include: swamps, bogs, fens, marshes, estuaries, tidal flats, ponds, shallow lakes, rivers and more, each supporting a diversity of species. Hippos and Nile crocodiles live in Africa, while anacondas are found in South America. Capybaras are from Central and South America, and flamingos live in the tropics. The rest of the animals in this book are found in North America. Moose and mallards also live in Europe, with some mallards found in Asia as well.

Wetlands are important ecosystems that are easily damaged by human activities, such as draining them to build homes or create farmland. As wetlands disappear, there is less habitat for wildlife. Today, conservationists are working hard to preserve wetlands around the world.